'Cardoness Castle', by William Daniell (1814).
(Courtesy of the National Library of Scotland.)

Cardoness Castle
and Carsluith Castle

Doreen Grove

Contents *Page*

Edited by Chris Tabraham
Illustrated by David Simon and Michelle McCluskie
Photography by Historic Scotland Photographic Unit

Printed in Scotland from sustainable material
by Buccleuch Printers Ltd., Hawick

First published by Historic Scotland 1996
Reprinted 2003

ISBN 1 900168 09 x

Introduction

"Cardines Towre standeth...harde upon
the watter of Flete: there can noo ordinance nor
gounes endomage yt of the sea, nor there canoo
artyllare be taken to it upon the lande...
At the ground eb men may ryde under the place
upoun the sandes one myle: and at the full sea,
boates of eight tonnes may come under the wall."

(AN ENGLISH SPY'S REPORT PREPARED FOR QUEEN
ELIZABETH OF ENGLAND BETWEEN 1563 AND 1566.)

Galloway is at the meeting-point of nations and cultures. It lies where Scotland meets Ireland, Man and England. Because of this it has a distinctive character and an equally fascinating history. The landscape of Galloway is one of upland moor and rocky shore. The Solway Firth determined its history, never more so than during the Middle Ages. Dotted along the deeply indented coastline are the ruins of many a fortified laird's house. Two of the finest are in State care ~ Cardoness and Carsluith.

The families associated with Cardoness and Carsluith were typical of the landed gentry in medieval Galloway. The McCullochs of Cardoness were of Gaelic descent; the Brouns of Carsluith had their origins in the Anglo-Norman lords encouraged into Galloway by the Crown during the twelfth century in an attempt to thwart the power of the independent Lords of Galloway. The two families differed in scale and importance: the McCullochs rubbed shoulders with the sovereign, while the Brouns never achieved high rank or great wealth. This is reflected in their lordly residences. Cardoness is a large and accomplished castle while Carsluith is a more modest tower house. But they are both on a par when it comes to giving the modern visitor insights into lordly life in medieval Galloway.

Cardoness Castle as it might have looked in 1500.

THE STORY OF CARDONESS CASTLE

THE LORDSHIP OF CARDONESS

The first mention of the family who took the name Cardoness is in 1220 when we read of Nicholas de Kerdenes and his wife Cicely being in dispute with the monastery at Dundrennan over Cicely's dowry. The litigation went on for more than 20 years. Nicholas was probably descended from David fitz Teri, Lord of Over Denton in Cumberland, who was in possession of Anwoth church (Cardoness is in Anwoth parish) by 1170.

The motte (left) and bailey (centre) at Boreland of Anwoth, built on a narrow promontory that once jutted out into the Water of Fleet a little to the west of Cardoness Castle. The place-name 'Boreland' meant the land that supported the lord's "board" or table.

David, son of Teri, was one of a number of Anglo-Norman lords tempted across the Solway Firth in the twelfth century from their Cumberland estates by the Crown in a determined effort to undermine the power of the independent Lords of Galloway. There was widespread unrest among the Gallovidians at their arrival which occasionally broke out into open revolt. The new Lords wisely built strong castles and most of these survive. David's residence, an unusual and well-preserved motte-and-bailey castle, can be seen behind the farmhouse of Boreland of Anwoth, a little to the west of Cardoness Castle.

The history of the family thereafter is vague. In 1277 Bertram of Cardonesss witnessed a charter by Lady Dervorguilla, of Buittle Castle near Dalbeattie, and mother of John Balliol who became King in 1292.

The McCullochs acquired Cardoness in the fifteenth century, possibly by marriage. Legend tells of the previous laird of Cardoness drowning in a frozen loch near the castle along with eight of his nine daughters as they celebrated the birth of his new-born son and heir, who also perished. The sole surviving daughter married a McCulloch from Wigtownshire. Gilbert McCulloch is the first to appear on record, as a witness to a charter in 1466. It was either Gilbert or his son, James, who built the present castle.

Cardoness Castle from the east.

The McCullochs of Cardoness

The McCullochs were already a powerful Galloway family by the time they came into possession of Cardoness. They appear in the records as a particularly lively family, frequently in dispute with their neighbours, particularly the Gordons, mostly over land ownership. James McCulloch of Cardoness (died 1500) resorted to litigation at least five times, once with his nearest neighbour. Nor was he a man of scruples, even where his family were concerned. He married off his only daughter to Alexander MacLellan, a 'natural idiot' apparently, so as to secure the curatorship of the young man's lands from his lawful curator, the Earl of Angus. The dispute lasted several years. Ninian, James' son, despite being a sheriff depute, seems to have had no more scruples than his father. He was prosecuted for breaking into a barn and stealing 1500 assorted beasts, and for taking rents illegally ~ all the property of his mother!

Ninian died in 1509, quite possibly executed for his crimes. His heir, Thomas, was a minor. This was the opportunity for the MacLellans to reclaim their rights and to prove a point. Patrick MacLellan, Alexander's brother, seized Cardoness in 1509, presumably not well defended, with little Thomas and his mother in the house.

Sir Alexander 'Sande' McCulloch had the wardship of Thomas from 1509 until his death on the battlefield of Flodden in 1513. He was clearly a friend of James IV, having been appointed keeper of Linlithgow Palace in 1505 and custodian of the King's falcons. His sporting interests also won him a wager of 35s from the King in the archery butts. But he too had the McCulloch talent for attracting trouble, and his two convictions against neighbours were only repealed after the King's intervention.

Sir Alexander's branch of the family was united with the Cardoness branch by the marriage of his daughter to young Alexander, who became laird on the death of his brother, Thomas, in 1516. Alexander was a typical McCulloch ~ soon in trouble. He is probably the 'Cutlar McCulloch' who led a raid in the early 1530s on the Isle of Man in retaliation for a raid by Lord Derby, the owner of that island, on Galloway. The McCullochs found it a lucrative venture and returned several times, giving rise to the Man proverb:

"God keep the good corn, the sheep, and the bullock,
From Satan, from sin, and from Cutlar M'Cullock."

The tower house at Cardoness cut open to show how the McCullochs might have made use of the accommodation.

CARDONESS AND THE THREAT FROM ENGLAND

Cardoness was built as the fortified house of the McCullochs. The perceived threat was from neighbouring families, with whom they were frequently in dispute, and not from a foreign power. The castle was therefore designed to withstand a lightly armed assault but not a fully pressed siege. However, the conflict with England in the 1540s and the civil war that followed Mary Queen of Scots' flight into exile in 1568 almost brought Cardoness onto the national stage.

An English spy drawing of Cruggleton Castle, across Wigtown Bay from Cardoness, drawn in about 1565, at the same time as the spy report on Cardoness was written.

Like many of the Gallovidian lairds, the McCullochs supported Mary Queen of Scots, at least until her defeat at Carberry Hill in 1567. By this date the strategic importance of Cardoness had been recognised for the castle had been included in a military report assessing the feasibility of an English army occupying the Scottish West March. The report, prepared by an English spy between 1563 and 1566, reads:

"Cardines Towre standeth upon an hight bancke and rocke, harde upoun the watter Flete: there can noo ordinance nor gounes endomage yt of the sea, nor there canoo artyllare be taken to it upoun the lande, ones having the house for the straitness of ground, and yf ye lande at Newton up upoun flete watter, then ye must pass one myle strait ground and up rockes, wheare noo ordinance can be caryed but upoun mens backes. Yt is nyne foote thick of the wall, without a bermeking, and withoute battaling. At the ground eb men may ryde under the place upoun the sandes one myle: And at the full sea, boates of eight tonnes may come under the wall. It may be taken with two hundreitht men, at the sudden. And being in Engliss possession, may be kepte with one hundreit men in garrisone: It will annoye the inhabitantes betuix the watter of Cree aforesaid, and Kiyrkcowbright; and be assistant to the same. Distant by see from Wirkington in Englonde tuenty-tuo myles."

The invasion never came about and the McCullochs returned to doing what they did best ~ feuding with their neighbours.

An 'inverted-keyhole' gun-hole in the tower house at Cardoness. The little holes in the left side of the vertical slit show that it had an outside shutter.

Dispute and Disgrace

The arms of Sir Godfrey McCulloch, 1672.

This constant feuding in time left the McCulloch finances in ruin. And it was the financial misdeeds of William McCulloch from 1592 onwards that eventually led to the mortgaging of the estate of Cardoness. By 1628 it was irredeemably lost to John Gordon of Upper Ardwall, a family with whom they had frequently feuded.

The McCullochs seem not to have recognised this change in their circumstances for by 1668 they were back at Cardoness. (The Gordons had evidently preferred to remain in their house, Bush o' Bield, near Anwoth, demolished in 1827.) Neither Alexander nor Godfrey, his son, appears to have accepted the Gordons' rights to the estate and both commited violent deeds in their attempts to win. The father was heavily fined for assaulting Marion Peebles, Gordon's widow, in 1668. The dreadful man dragged her from her sick bed, out of the house and onto a dung-heap where he left her to die. The son shot and fatally wounded Gordon himself at Bush o'Bield, a crime for which he was sentenced to death. He escaped abroad for several years but was spotted soon after his return, ironically while attending a church service in St Giles in Edinburgh. He was executed in the capital, one of the last to perish on 'The Maiden'~ the Scottish equivalent of the guillotine.

The house of Bush o' Bield before it was demolished in 1827.

With Godfrey's death Cardoness was abandoned and a different form of wildlife took up residence:

"Sae in the tower o' Cardoness
A howlet sits at noon"
(*Election Ballads*, by Robert Burns)

The castle then passed through several hands ~ the Gordons, the Maxwells, the Stewarts, the Murray-Baillies of Cally, and back to the Maxwells. It was Lady Maxwell who placed the castle in State care in 1927.

A SHORT TOUR O

1. PROMONTORY

A NATURAL ROCKY HEADLAND, THE IDEAL SITE FOR A CASTLE. BEFORE THE MEANDERING FLEET ESTUARY WAS CANALISED IN 1824 FOR AGRICULTURAL IMPROVEMENTS, THE SEA LAPPED RIGHT UP AGAINST THE PROMONTORY AT HIGH TIDE.

2. COURTYARD

THE FLAT PLATEAU ON THE SOUTH SIDE OF THE TOWER HOUSE [4], WITH OUTBUILDINGS [3] AROUND THE CENTRAL OPEN SPACE. THE COURTYRAD IS NOW DEFINED BY A LOW WALL. THE SMALL SQUARE BUILDING BESIDE THE SITE OF THE ENTRANCE WAS PROBABLY A PORTER'S LODGE.

2

3

CARDONESS CASTLE

3. OUTBUILDINGS

THE EXISTING STONE-VAULTED BUILDINGS WERE RECONSTRUCTED IN THE 1920s AFTER EXCAVATIONS REVEALED THE FOUNDATIONS OF VARIOUS STRUCTURES. THEIR FUNCTIONS ARE NOT KNOWN BUT THEY WOULD HAVE COMPLEMENTED THE RESIDENTIAL AND SERVICE ACCOMMODATION IN THE TOWER HOUSE [4], EG OUTER HALL, KITCHEN, STORAGE CELLARS AND STABLES.

4. TOWER HOUSE

THE MAIN BUILDING IN THE CASTLE, HOUSING THE LODGINGS FOR THE LAIRD, HIS FAMILY AND PERSONAL SERVANTS. THE STONE-VAULTED BASEMENT ON TWO FLOORS WAS FOR STORES AND CONTAINED A GRIM PIT-PRISON. THE SECOND FLOOR WAS THE HALL, THE PUBLIC ROOM, WITH THE LAIRD'S PRIVATE APARTMENT ON THE TOP FLOORS.

Artist's bird's-eye view of the castle from the north west.

THE ARCHITECTURE OF CARDONESS CASTLE

THE CASTLE AS A DEFENCE

The natural **promontory** on which Cardoness Castle stands was its best defence. Even today, despite all the changes done by Alexander Murray of Broughton, MP, in the 1820s to drain the Fleet estuary for agricultural improvements, the visitor can appreciate why the McCullochs chose this location for their new castle in the later fifteenth century.

The natural defences were not lost on the English spy who drew up his account of the castle in the mid-sixteenth century (see page 9). He estimated that, even without a barmkin (defensive outer wall) and battlements, the castle would need 200 men to capture it.

The castle was built at a time when the new-fangled gunpowdered artillery was beginning to rival the conventional weaponry (stone-throwing machines, long- and cross-bows). Hence the tower house is well provided with **gun-holes**, of the 'inverted-keyhole' type then in vogue, making Cardoness one of the earliest castles in Scotland to make provision for guns in its construction.

In almost all other respects the tower house at Cardoness is typical of other Scottish tower houses regarding its defence. The walls are 2.5 m thick and the openings are few and far between. The only **entrance** into the tower is through the arched doorway in the south wall which has evidence for two barriers, an outer oak door and an inner iron 'yett' (cross-barred gate). Inside the doorway is a hole in the ceiling, called a '**murder-hole**' because it could well have been used by the defending garrison to drop unpleasant things onto intruders. It probably saw more use as a means of moving objects between floors. A **guardroom** or porter's lodge lies just to the left of the entrance.

In one important defensive respect the tower house is unusual. There is no sign of battlements (a defended wall-head) at the wall-tops, confirming the English spy's observation that by the 1560s there were none. It is most unlikely that no battlements were provided in the original construction for in the later fifteenth century we would expect to find the main part of the defence being carried on from the wall-head. It may be that the remodelling of the upper storeys resulted in this defensive element being removed by the 1560s. The original battlements, if they existed, would have given the McCullochs the most excellent views across the Solway Firth and out towards the Isle of Man.

The tower house at Cardoness from the south-west. The buildings in front were rebuilt to the present state in the early 1930s.

The Castle as a Residence

The castle was the residence of a wealthy and well-to-do nobleman. It had, therefore, to be capable of serving a number of functions ~ private residence, estate office, law court and guest-house. Only the tower house survives more or less complete. This was chiefly the laird's private lodging, but housing also some storage space and the prison. The other accommodation needs ~ including an outer hall (for meetings of the tenantry, large-scale banqueting and the like), kitchen, storage cellars, stables, bakehouse and brewhouse ~ were sited to the south of the tower house around the courtyard. The **stone-vaulted buildings** there now were largely reconstructed in the 1930s and little can usefully be said about their medieval form and function.

A cut-open reconstruction of the entrance and lower levels of the tower house showing the 'murder-hole', the storage cellars and the grim prison and pit.

The storage cellars.

The dour simplicity of the exterior of the tower house belies the well-planned interior where every space was used to good advantage. The tower house contained six storeys of accommodation. The family's private lodgings were on the top three floors and storage provision in the bottom two. Sandwiched between was the hall, the 'public' room in the tower.

The **ground floor** was formerly divided into two **storage cellars** by a cross-wall which has now gone, though the two entrance doors survive. The larger, west cellar has a slop-sink under the gun-hole in the north wall and two unusual circular recesses in the west wall. These were probably used for storage of some sort, perhaps pickling or salting tubs.

The corbel-stones projecting from the side walls carried the timber joists of a loft, or entresol, also used for **storage**. It is featureless save for a small window in the west wall flanked by two small cupboards. It was entered through an arched door in the east wall, reached from the **spiral stair** in the south-east corner of the building, which provides the only access to the upper chambers. Also at this level are two **wall chambers**. The one directly over the entrance contains the 'murder-hole'. The chamber in the east wall was a **prison and pit**. The upper cell has a latrine in the north wall and a narrow window; the trap-door in the floor gives access to a dark, dank pit-prison below.

The **first floor** contained just one large room, the **hall**, the public room in the tower. It was used for more intimate entertaining and feasting, to complement the larger outer hall in the courtyard. It has been a handsome room, well lit through two beautifully proportioned windows furnished with stone benches. The quality of the masonry is best seen in the finely carved cupboards in the side walls and the capacious fireplace (now lacking its massive stone lintel) in the north wall with a salt-box in its right-hand jamb. **Four wall chambers** open off the hall, the one in the north wall having been the **latrine-closet.**

The hall on the first floor and (above) the upper chamber on the second floor. Each room originally occupied the whole floor and was heated by a splendid fireplace. The upper chamber was later subdivided into two by the construction of the cross-wall at the top of the photograph.

The hall fireplace, now missing its stone lintel, with (left) a fine aumbry, or cupboard, once fitted with shelves, and (right) the salt-box, once fitted with doors.

The **floors over the hall** are now without their wooden floors and are more difficult to inspect. Together they provided the **private lodgings** for the laird's family and personal servants. The **floor immediately above the hall** was originally one large room like the hall. This was the **great chamber**, the family's withdrawing room. It was originally entered through the arched door (blocked in the subsequent reorganisation) in the east wall. It was heated by the elaborate fireplace in the west wall, with a salt-box in its left-hand jamb. The **one wall chamber** in the north-east corner was the **latrine-closet**. At a later date the room was divided into two smaller chambers, each entered through a doorway at the end of a passage formed in the south wall. A modest fireplace was inserted in the east chamber. Moulded corbel-stones and joist-holes on the west wall indicate the floor levels of the **chambers and attic above**. These provided additional private rooms for the family.

The Story of Carsluith Castle

Carsluith Castle was built in the fifteenth century by the Cairns family. In 1422, Alexander de Cairns, provost of Lincluden and a distinguished follower of Archibald, fourth Earl of Douglas, gifted Carsluith to his nephew, John Cairns of Orchardton. In 1506, the land passed to Lindsay of Fairgirth as a dowry when he married Margaret Cairns. The story was repeated in the next generation when Elizabeth Lindsay married Richard Broun of Lands Farm, New Abbey. Thereafter Carsluith is associated with this family.

The Brouns' Gallovidian origins are obscure. One of their number was certainly in Galloway in the early twelfth century, as an official of David I during the establishment of Dundrennan Abbey. By the end of the thirteenth century the Brouns, in common with most Gallovidians, were supporting John Balliol's cause. During the wars with England that followed Balliol's removal from the throne in 1296, several members of the family were captured and imprisoned. By the late fifteenth century various members of the family owned estates across Galloway. Both the Brouns and the Cairnses held their lands from the Church. Like the McCullochs of Cardoness the Brouns were affected by the lawlessness of the time. In one episode, John Broun, son of the laird, was arrested for his part in the murder of James McCulloch of Barholm.

The Brouns' most famous son was Gilbert Broun, the last abbot of Sweetheart Abbey, who may have been born at Carsluith. He became a scholar of note. Lord Scrope, the English warden of the West March, wrote that "*yt is thought that he is very learned, havinge bestowed 4 or 5 years at Oxford*". Gilbert, having come to the Church late, took Holy Orders just at the time when the Scottish Church was in crisis. By the time of the Reformation in 1560 he was abbot of Sweatheart and fought the Reformation tooth and nail. He fortified his abbey and went on performing services despite threats against him. Eventually in 1606 he was arrested and imprisoned in Blackness Castle, on the Firth of Forth. Despite his advancing years and failing health he managed to escape to France and by 1608 was back at his abbey where he was arrested once again. The authorities were persuaded to ward the aging cleric in his own monastery after sureties were given for his good behaviour. The abbot was not having that. In the following year a search of his chambers revealed "*a great number of books, copes, chalices, pictures, images and such other*

Popish trash". The articles were destroyed and Gilbert expelled. He fled to France, to die in Paris a very old man.

Carsluith Castle stayed with the Brouns until 1748 when James Broun, by now a druggist and merchant in London, sold the estate to Alexander Johnston prior to sailing for India. The lands passed through several hands before coming into State care in 1913.

Carsluith Castle as it might have looked in 1600.

THE ARCHITECTURE OF CARSLUITH CASTLE

Carsluith Castle is a lightly-defended tower house, typical of the many L-planned tower houses built by the landed gentry throughout the country after the Reformation of the 1560s. Carsluith, however, has a more complicated building history than most for it seems to have begun life as a simple oblong tower in the late fifteenth or early sixteenth century. The present **stair-tower**, by which the main house is reached, was added in 1568. The date, together with a motto (now almost illegible), the arms of Broun (a chevron between three fleurs-de-lis), and the letter 'B', are carved on the **panel above the entrance doorway.** The secondary nature of the stair-tower is indicated, among other things, by the awkward way in which the projecting top storey of the stair-tower runs into an old window recess in the re-entrant angle.

The arms of the Brouns of Carsluith.

Carsluith Castle from the north-east.

The addition of the stair-tower increased the accommodation in the house and improved the circulation through it. It was accompanied by other works. These probably included the removal of the wall-head battlements along the north and south walls. A novel and attractive change was the construction of a timber gallery or balcony on the outside of the north wall. This was entered from the second floor of the main block through an original window enlarged to form a door, and through a door off the main stair (later converted into a window). Three projecting stone corbels supporting the sloping roof survive. The hint of the

The water-spout at the south-west corner of Carsluith carved in the form of a human face.

balcony, and the presence of charming little details like the carved face on the water-spout at the south-west corner, make this a delightful house to visit.

The tower house has four storeys of accommodation. At **ground level** are **two storage cellars**, both stone-vaulted to reduce the risk of fire and give greater stability to the lofty building. Both cellars have a strange window arrangement, one small window over another. This may be an alteration to improve the lighting.

The **first floor** was one large room, the **hall.** The focal point of the hall was the large moulded fireplace in the north wall. It has a salt-box in the left-hand jamb. The hall is well lit by windows in each wall. There is a slop-sink at the south-west corner and a wall-closet in the north-west angle, possibly a latrine-closet.

The hall on the first floor of Carsluith Castle as it might have been used in 1600.

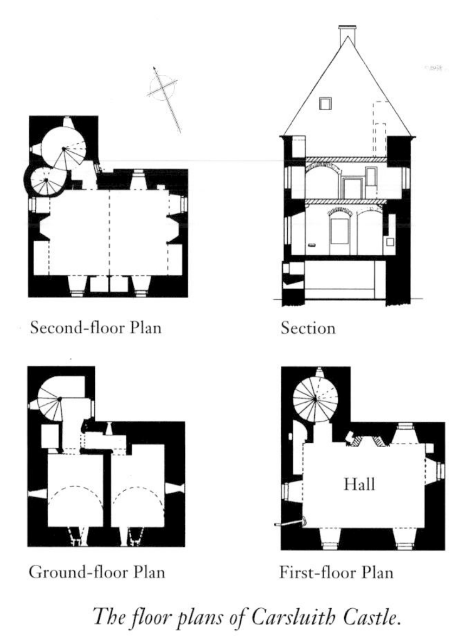

The floor plans of Carsluith Castle.

The **second floor** was originally divided by a timber partition into two rooms to form the laird's **private apartment.** One would have contained his great four-poster bed. Each has a fireplace, a latrine-closet and good-sized windows (though these have been enlarged at a later date). The north window in the east room was converted into a doorway, possibly when the stair-tower was added in 1568. It gave access to the balcony mentioned above.

The top floor and the rooms above the main stair, reached by a small stair in the thickness of the wall, provided extra private chambers for the family.

Further Reading

On Cardoness Castle:

D MacGibbon & T Ross *The Castellated and Domestic Architecture of Scotland*, 1 (1887), 243-7

J Fleming *Cardoness Castle* (1909)

W McCulloch of Ardwell *A History of the Galloway McCullochs* (1964)

Royal Commission on the Ancient and Historical Monuments of Scotland *Inventory of Kirkcudbrightshire* (1914)

On Carsluith Castle:

D MacGibbon & T Ross *The Castellated and Domestic Architecture of Scotland*, 3 (1889), 513-5

Royal Commission on the Ancient and Historical Monuments of Scotland *Inventory of Kirkcudbrightshire* (1914)

On Castles Generally:

S Cruden *The Scottish Castle* (1981)

C Tabraham *Scottish Castles and Fortifications* (1990)

C Tabraham *Scotland's Castles* (1997)